Howard A. Rose

Create Journal Publishing

COPYRIGHT © 2020 By Howard Rose
All Rights reserved. No part of this book may be reproduced without written permission of the copyright owner except for the use of quotations in a book review.

My Million Dollar Idea   Date_____

Idea:_____

List the 10 most important things that need to be: learned, organized, studied, solved, figured out... to get this project/idea off the ground and start to become a reality.

1._____
_____
2._____
_____
3._____
_____
4._____
_____
5._____
_____
6._____
_____
7._____
_____
8._____
_____
9._____
_____
10._____
_____

Name:_____

My Million Dollar Idea

My Million Dollar Idea

My Million Dollar Idea

My Million Dollar Idea

My Million Dollar Idea

My Million Dollar Idea

My Million Dollar Idea

My Million Dollar Idea

My Million Dollar Idea

My Million Dollar Idea

My Million Dollar Idea

My Million Dollar Idea

My Million Dollar Idea

My Million Dollar Idea

My Million Dollar Idea

My Million Dollar Idea

My Million Dollar Idea

My Million Dollar Idea

My Million Dollar Idea

My Million Dollar Idea

My Million Dollar Idea

My Million Dollar Idea

My Million Dollar Idea

My Million Dollar Idea

My Million Dollar Idea

My Million Dollar Idea

My Million Dollar Idea

My Million Dollar Idea

My Million Dollar Idea

My Million Dollar Idea

My Million Dollar Idea

My Million Dollar Idea

My Million Dollar Idea

My Million Dollar Idea

My Million Dollar Idea

My Million Dollar Idea

My Million Dollar Idea

My Million Dollar Idea

My Million Dollar Idea

My Million Dollar Idea

My Million Dollar Idea

My Million Dollar Idea

My Million Dollar Idea

My Million Dollar Idea

My Million Dollar Idea

My Million Dollar Idea

My Million Dollar Idea

My Million Dollar Idea

My Million Dollar Idea

My Million Dollar Idea

My Million Dollar Idea

My Million Dollar Idea

My Million Dollar Idea

My Million Dollar Idea

My Million Dollar Idea

My Million Dollar Idea

My Million Dollar Idea

My Million Dollar Idea

My Million Dollar Idea

My Million Dollar Idea

My Million Dollar Idea

My Million Dollar Idea

My Million Dollar Idea

My Million Dollar Idea

My Million Dollar Idea

My Million Dollar Idea

My Million Dollar Idea

My Million Dollar Idea

My Million Dollar Idea

My Million Dollar Idea

My Million Dollar Idea

My Million Dollar Idea

My Million Dollar Idea

My Million Dollar Idea

My Million Dollar Idea

My Million Dollar Idea

My Million Dollar Idea

My Million Dollar Idea

My Million Dollar Idea

My Million Dollar Idea

My Million Dollar Idea

My Million Dollar Idea

My Million Dollar Idea

My Million Dollar Idea

My Million Dollar Idea

My Million Dollar Idea

My Million Dollar Idea

My Million Dollar Idea

My Million Dollar Idea

My Million Dollar Idea

My Million Dollar Idea

My Million Dollar Idea

My Million Dollar Idea

My Million Dollar Idea

My Million Dollar Idea

My Million Dollar Idea

My Million Dollar Idea

My Million Dollar Idea

My Million Dollar Idea

My Million Dollar Idea

My Million Dollar Idea

My Million Dollar Idea

www.ingramcontent.com/pod-product-compliance
Lightning Source LLC
Chambersburg PA
CBHW071423210526
45465CB00001B/503